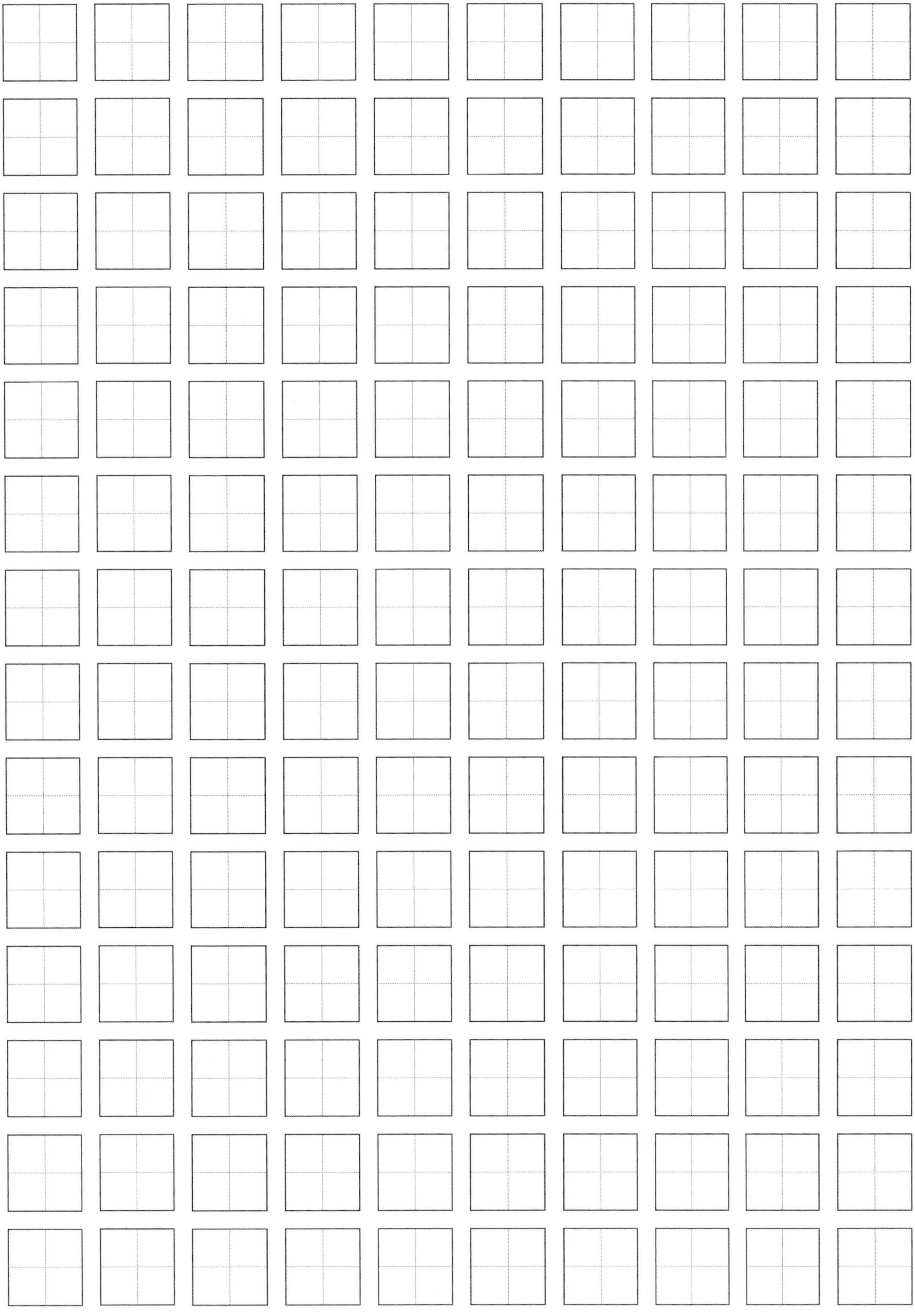

Made in United States
North Haven, CT
02 October 2023

42254794R00067